Creative CAT Crafts

Get Crafty with Pets!

All Crafts in This Book Were
CAT TESTED AND **CAT APPROVED**

Jane Yates

Gareth Stevens
PUBLISHING

Published in 2019 by Gareth Stevens,
an Imprint of Rosen Publishing
29 East 21st Street, New York, NY 10010

Developed and produced for Rosen by BlueAppleWorks Inc.

Creative Director: Melissa McClellan
Managing Editor for BlueAppleWorks: Melissa McClellan
Designer: T.J. Choleva
Photo Research: Jane Reid
Editor: Marcia Abramson

Craft Artisans: Sarah Hodgins (p. 12, 14); Jane Yates (p. 8, 10, 16, 18, 20, 22, 24, 26, 28)

Photo Credits: © cover center Cressida studio/Shutterstock.com; cover top left My head/Shutterstock.com; cover top right Tony Campbell/Dreamstime; cover middle right Austen Photography; cover bottom right Okssi/Shutterstock.com; Paw print Dreamzdesigners/Shutterstock.com; p. 4 left Ivan Kovbasniuk/Dreamstime; p 4 top right Maryna Kulchytska/Shutterstock.com; p. 4 top right middle Ruth Black/Dreamstime; p. 4 bottom right middle BlurryMe/Shutterstock.com; p. 4 bottom right Nina Buday/Shutterstock.com; p. 5 top left Criastian Filip/Dreamstime ; p. 5 middle left Karen-Richards/Shutterstock.com; p. 5 bottom left luckyraccoon/Shutterstock.com; p. 5 top right Kuttelvaserova Stuchelova/Shutterstock.com; p. 5 bottom right Grigorita Ko/Shutterstock.com; p. 6 left Isselee/Dreamstime; p. 8 Vladimir Voronin/Dreamstime; p. 9 Myrchella/Dreamstime.com p. 10 top Andreykuzmin/Dreamstime.com; p. 11 bottom right Photodeti/Dreamstime.com; p. 13 middle matin/Shutterstock.com; p. 13 bottom right Khomulo Anna/Shutterstock.com; p. 16 bottom right MyImages - Micha/Shutterstock.com; p. 18 top Kakca22/Dreamstime; p. 18 bottom right Olena Sushytska/Dreamstime; p. 21 bottom right Irina oxilixo Danilova/Shutterstock.com; p. 23 middle right Ksena2009/Dreamstime; p. 25 Vadim Usov/Dreamstime; p. 27 middle right Vitaly Titov/Shutterstock.com; p. 29 bottom right Evgenyi/Shutterstock.com; p. 31 Erik Lam/Dreamstime; p. 32 left Peter Wollinga/Shutterstock.com; p. 32 right robert_s/Shutterstock.com; back cover left to right: Austen Photography; Myrchella/Dreamstime; Austen Photography; Evgenyi/Shutterstock.com; All craft photography Austen Photography

Cataloging-in-Publication-Data
Names: Yates, Jane.
Title: Creative cat crafts / Jane Yates.
Description: New York : Gareth Stevens Publishing, 2019. | Series: Get crafty with pets! | Includes glossary and index.
Identifiers: LCCN ISBN 9781538226117 (pbk.) | ISBN 9781538226100 (library bound) | ISBN 9781538226124 (6 pack)
Subjects: LCSH: Handicraft--Juvenile literature. | Cats--Juvenile literature. | Cats in art--Juvenile literature. | Pets--Juvenile literature. | Pet supplies--Juvenile literature.
Classification: LCC TT160.Y38 2019 | DDC 745.59--dc23

Manufactured in the United States of America

CPSIA Compliance Information: Batch #CS18GS For Further Information contact: Rosen Publishing, New York, New York at 1-800-237-9932

Contents

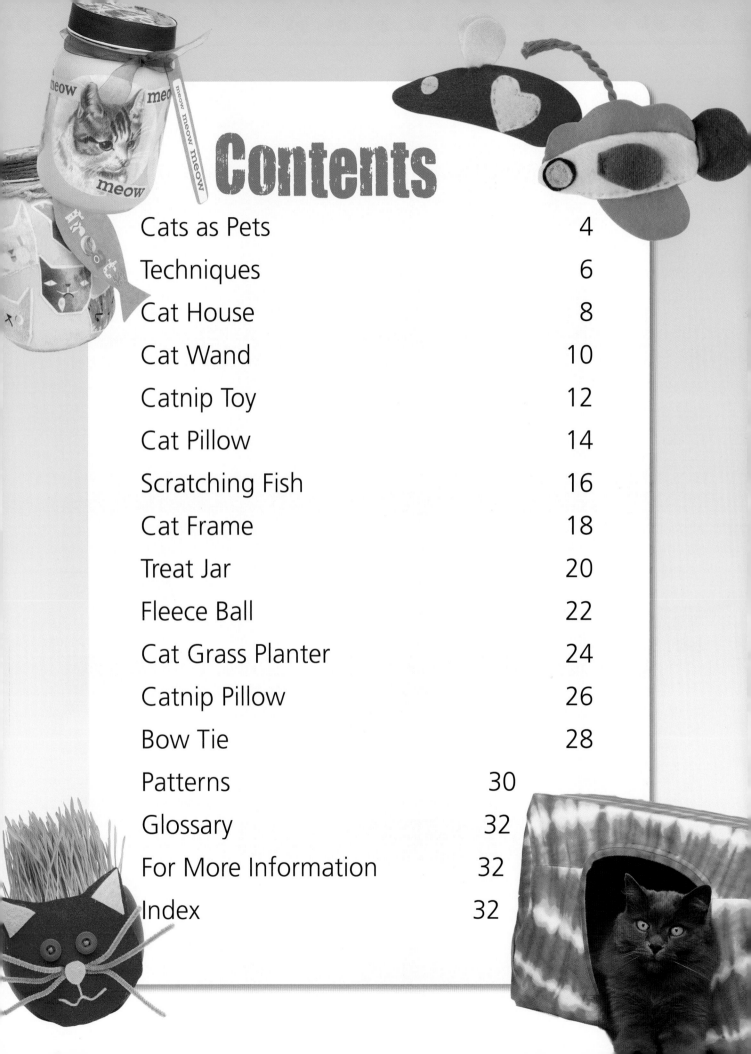

Cats as Pets

Our furry four-legged companions are miniature versions of wild cats. They weren't **domesticated** so much as they decided they liked hanging around people. While many will do a job such as killing rodents, you can't count on it.

Cats are among the most popular pets in the world today, with as many as 74 million cats living in U.S. homes. Cats like attention, they like to be petted and cuddled, and they like to play. They can even be trained to do tricks with a lot of **perseverance**. Cats are very thoughtful and intelligent. Cats make wonderful pets and are loving and endlessly entertaining.

Cats are good friends. You have to earn their trust and love by treating them with kindness and taking good care of them.

CATS MAKE US HAPPY

CATS PURR WHEN HAPPY

CATS LOVE TO CUDDLE

CAT PHOTOGRAPHY

You might want to take pictures of your pet cat and use them for some craft projects. Read the tips below and try taking pictures of cats.

Make sure your pet feels comfortable. Instead of bringing your cat to you, go to where your cat likes to be. Get down on the ground to take photos on the animal's level—don't take all the photos from above. It's best to take the photos outside or near a window. Use treats and your pet's favorite toys to get your cat's attention. Take lots of pictures from different angles.

EYE LEVEL

CLOSE-UP

HIGH ANGLE

ACTION

LOW ANGLE

PHOTO TIP
Have someone stand beside you with a treat or a cat toy to get the cat to look at the camera.

Techniques

These projects are great for cat lovers whether you have a cat or hope to have a cat in the future (make the toys and save them in a cat **hope chest**). They also make great gifts for someone you know who has a cat.
Most of the materials in this book can be easily found. You may have some already. Others can can be purchased at craft or dollar stores.
Use the following techniques to create your crafts.

PAPER-MACHE GLUE

> Add equal amounts of white glue and water in a bowl. Mix the glue and water together with a spoon. If you have leftover glue, put it in a container with a lid and use it later. (An empty yogurt container works well.)

THREADING A NEEDLE

> Use a tapestry needle for working with yarn. Use a needle with a smaller opening for working with thread.

> Wet one end of the thread in your mouth. Poke it through the needle opening. Pull some of the thread through until you have an even amount and make a double knot.

Put the thread through the loop.

> For yarn, fold a piece of yarn over, then push the fold through the opening. This is easier than using a single thread.

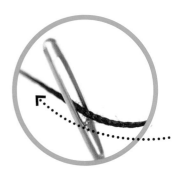

Fold the yarn, then feed it through the loop.

A NOTE ABOUT MEASUREMENTS

Measurements are given in U.S. form with metric in parentheses. For fractions like ¼ inch, a less-than-whole metric number is given to make it easier to measure.

Overcast Stitch

› Thread a needle, then tie a knot at the other end.

› Place the needle and knotted thread in between the two pieces of cloth. Push the needle through the top layer. Pull the thread through so the knot is hidden in between the layers.

› Loop the needle around the edges of the cloth. Push the needle through both layers of cloth to make your first full stitch.

› Angle the needle toward the spot where the next stitch will be.

› Continue stitching until finished.

Using Patterns

› Patterns help you cut out exact shapes when making crafts.

› Use tape or pins to attach the pattern to the cloth before you start cutting.

› When cutting out a shape, cut around the shape first, then make smaller cuts.

› When cutting with scissors, move the piece of cloth instead of the scissors.

› Make sure you keep your fingers out of the way while cutting. Ask an adult for help if needed.

Trace the pattern.

Cut the pattern out.

Attach the pattern to the cloth.

Cut the cloth along the pattern lines.

BE PREPARED

› Read through the instructions and make sure you have all the materials you need.

› Clean up when you are finished making your crafts. Put away your supplies for next time.

BE SAFE

› Ask for help when you need it.

› Ask for permission to borrow tools.

› Be careful when using scissors and needles.

cat House

Make a cat house using an old T-shirt and box. Warning: your cat may want to help you make it.

Tools & Materials:

- ✔ Large cardboard box
- ✔ T-shirt (adult large or bigger)
- ✔ Safety pins
- ✔ Soft blanket or pillow

1 Find a large cardboard box big enough for your cat to fit inside of. If it has top flaps, have an adult remove them.

2 Stretch the T-shirt over the box so that the neck opening is over the open end of the box.

3 Pull the fabric so that the neck opening is centered over the open side and the bottom of the shirt is pulled to the back.

4 Tuck the sleeves in and use a safety pin to secure them.

5 Pull the bottom ends of the shirt together and use safety pins to secure.

6 Put a nice soft blanket or pillow inside.

2 Pull T-shirt over box

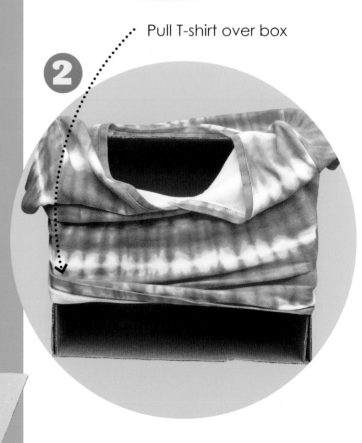

Remove flaps

1

3 ····· Pull tight

4 Pin ·····
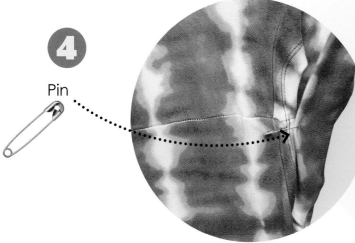

5 Pin   Pin   Pin
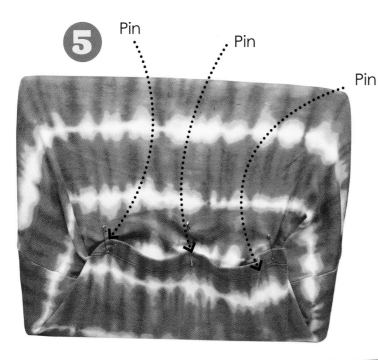

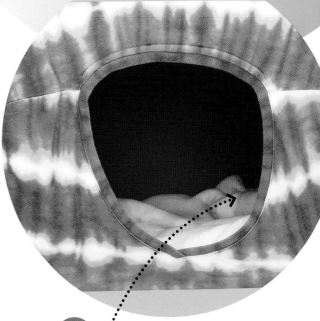

6 ····· Add blanket

9

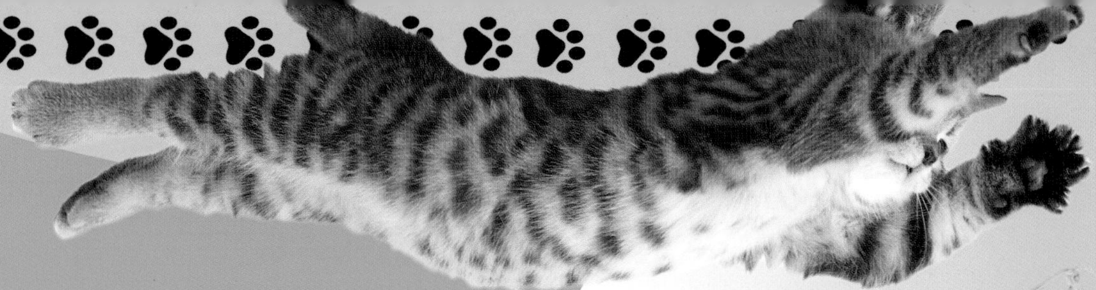

Cat Wand

A cat wand is a great way to encourage a cat to play. It will not be able to resist chasing the feathers as you swing the wand.

Tools & Materials:

✔ Paint and paintbrush
✔ 36-inch (91 cm) × 1/4-inch (.6 cm) dowel
✔ 24-inch (61 cm) piece of string
✔ Tape
✔ 4 craft feathers
✔ Paper clip

1 Paint the dowel and leave to dry.

2 Wrap the string around one end of the dowel several times and tie a double knot.

3 Wrap tape around the string and end of the dowel.

4 Gather four feathers together. Wrap tape around the tips.

5 Tape a large paper clip to the feathers. Leave one end uncovered.

6 Tie the end of the string taped to the dowel to the paper clip. Wrap the string around the paper clip several times and then tie a double knot.

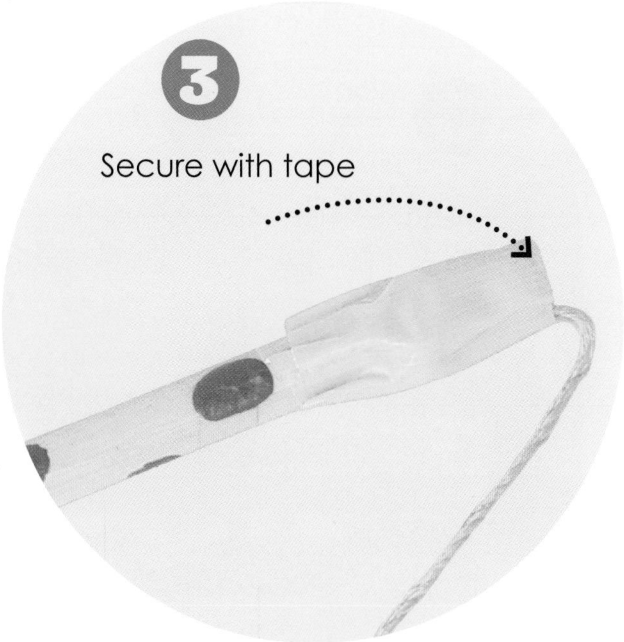

3 Secure with tape

2 Tie

4

Tape

Another IDEA!

Instead of using feathers, tape a bunch of 12-inch (30 cm) pieces of ribbons together. Tape a paper clip to the ribbons and attach to the dowel. You could also use a small catnip toy or a strip of fleece.

5

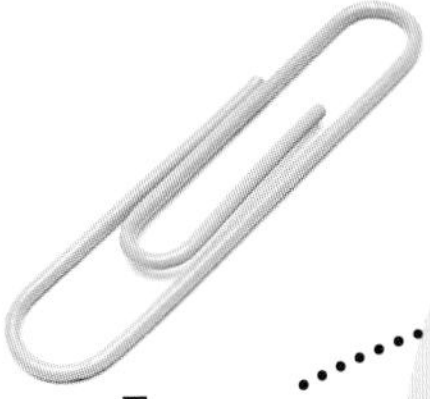

Tape

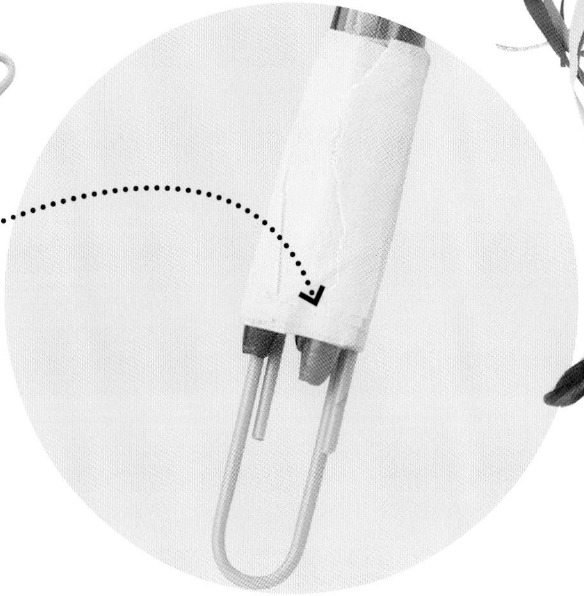

Did You Know?

When cats live outside, they chase prey, climb, and jump. Indoor cats need to do the same things to stay healthy. A cat wand is a great way to encourage your cat to exercise. It is also a great way to interact and have fun with your cat.

Make a knot

6

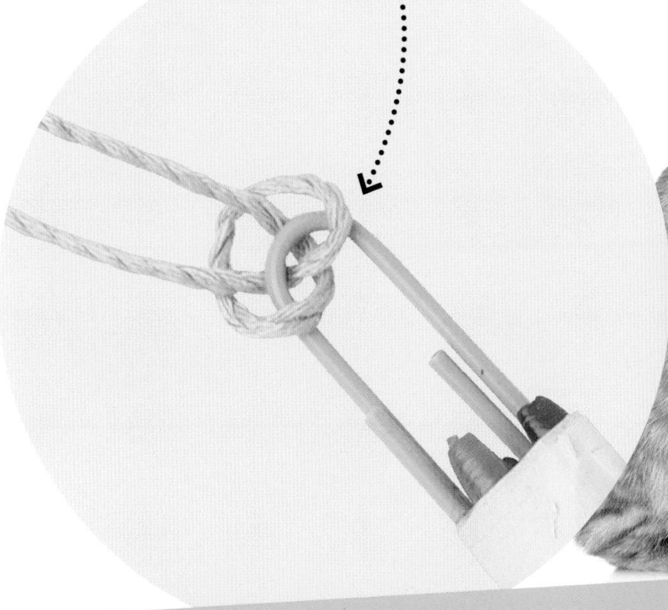

TIP

Put the wand away when you're finished playing so your cat doesn't chew on the string.

Catnip Toy

Make cute catnip toys with felt. Catnip is a dried herb that most cats love.

Tools & Materials:

- ✔ Paper, pencil, and scissors
- ✔ Felt in a variety of colors
- ✔ Sewing needle and thread
- ✔ Straight pins
- ✔ Catnip

1 Trace the fish template parts on page 30 on paper and cut each piece out.

2 Trace the pieces onto your chosen colors of felt. Cut four circles for the eyes (two larger circles and two smaller circles), two body pieces, and two side fins.

3 Sew one large eye circle and one smaller eye circle to each side of the fish body. Sew a side fin piece to each body piece. Sew the tail to one piece.

4 On one of the body pieces, pin the top fin to the edge, matching edges. Sew into place, close to the edge. Turn your fish body upside down and repeat for the bottom fin.

5 Place the two fish body pieces together (the eyes, fins, and tail will all be on the inside). Make sure all the fins are very well tucked inside. Pin all around but leave a small opening on the bottom.

6 Sew around the fish body pieces starting at the opening until you reach the other side of the opening. Remove the pins. Turn the fish right side out.

7 Fill the fish with catnip through the opening at the bottom of your fish. Sew the opening closed.

Trace and cut ·············

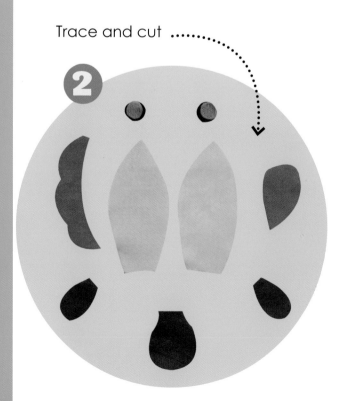

3

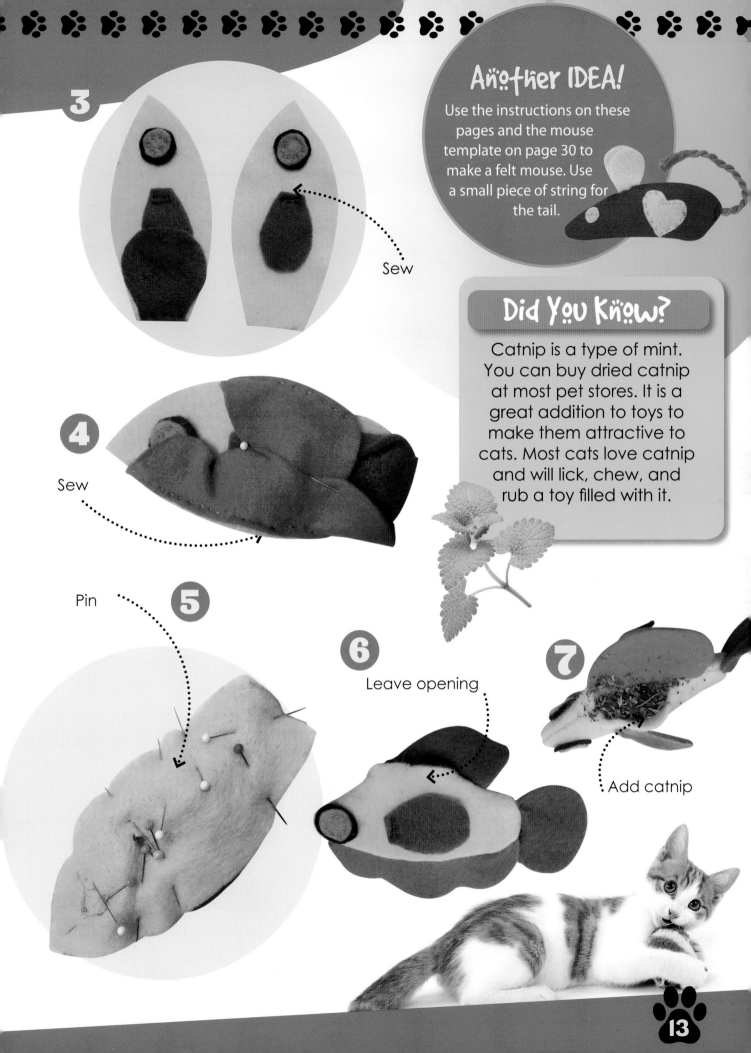

Sew

Another IDEA!

Use the instructions on these pages and the mouse template on page 30 to make a felt mouse. Use a small piece of string for the tail.

Did You Know?

Catnip is a type of mint. You can buy dried catnip at most pet stores. It is a great addition to toys to make them attractive to cats. Most cats love catnip and will lick, chew, and rub a toy filled with it.

4

Sew

5

Pin

6

Leave opening

7

Add catnip

Cat Pillow

Make an adorable cat pillow to put on your bed or favorite chair.

Tools & Materials:
- ✔ Large piece of paper
- ✔ Pencil and scissors
- ✔ Large piece of fabric
- ✔ Felt in a variety of colors
- ✔ 2 buttons
- ✔ Yarn, thread, and needles
- ✔ Marker (optional)
- ✔ Fabric stuffing

1 Trace the circle template from page 30 on paper and cut it out. Trace the circle onto a piece of folded fabric. Cut the fabric circles out.

2 Cut two small circles in one color of felt and two smaller circles in another color of felt for eyes.

3 Cut a small triangle for the nose.

4 Cut two medium circles from felt for the cheeks. Cut 10 strands of yarn. Sew five to each circle.

5 Place the eye circles on the front of one large pillow circle. Sew into place. Sew two buttons on top of the little circles. Sew the nose below the eyes. Sew the cheeks on. Draw a mouth with a permanent marker or sew a mouth using yarn and a darning needle.

6 Make ears: Cut two triangles out of felt. Cut two smaller triangles from another color of felt. Sew the smaller triangles to the larger triangles.

7 To attach the ears, place them on the top of the front of the pillow upside down and sew them to the front of the pillow close to the edge.

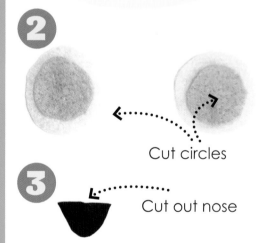

2 Cut circles

3 Cut out nose

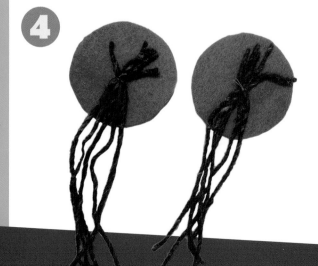

4

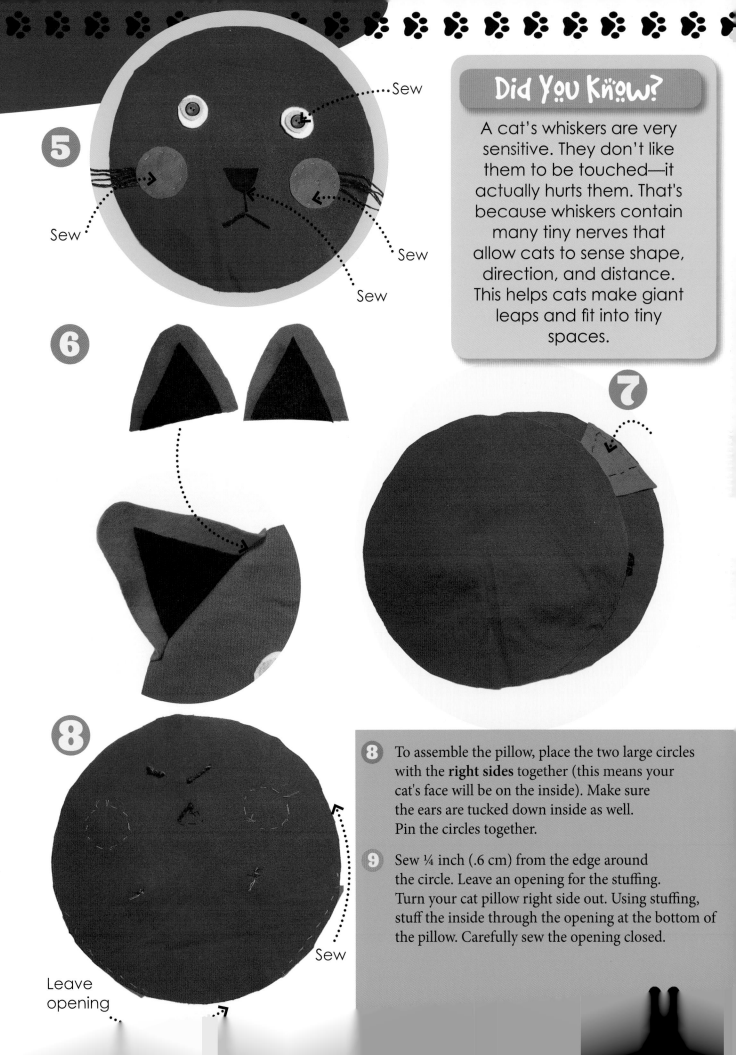

5 Sew · · · · · · · · · · · ·

Sew · · · · · · · · ·

Sew · · · · · · · · ·

Sew · · · · · · · · ·

6

7

8

Leave opening · · · · · ·

Sew · · · · ·

8 To assemble the pillow, place the two large circles with the **right sides** together (this means your cat's face will be on the inside). Make sure the ears are tucked down inside as well. Pin the circles together.

9 Sew ¼ inch (.6 cm) from the edge around the circle. Leave an opening for the stuffing. Turn your cat pillow right side out. Using stuffing, stuff the inside through the opening at the bottom of the pillow. Carefully sew the opening closed.

Scratching Fish

Make a scratching fish to hang on your door.

Tools & Materials:

- ✔ 2 pieces of thick cardboard
- ✔ Pencil, scissors, and nail
- ✔ 8-inch (20 cm) piece of string
- ✔ Glue
- ✔ Seagrass or sisal
- ✔ Markers (optional)

1 Draw a fish shape on one piece of the cardboard and cut it out.

2 Place this fish shape on your second piece of cardboard. Trace around it. Cut this fish shape out.

3 Poke a hole with a nail through one piece near the pointed end. Place this piece on top of the other one and punch a hole through the second piece.

4 Glue the two fish shapes together. Thread both ends of the string through the hole at one end of the fish shape. Make a double knot.

5 Tape one end of the seagrass to the bottom and back side of the fish shape. (The side with the string knot is the front.)

6 Turn the fish over. Spread some glue on the cardboard. Start wrapping the seagrass around the fish. Do it as tightly as you can. When you reach the end of the glue apply more. Press the seagrass into the glue. When you get to the top, cut the seagrass and tape the end to the back.

7 Optional: decorate the fish with markers.

2

Trace the fish shape

16

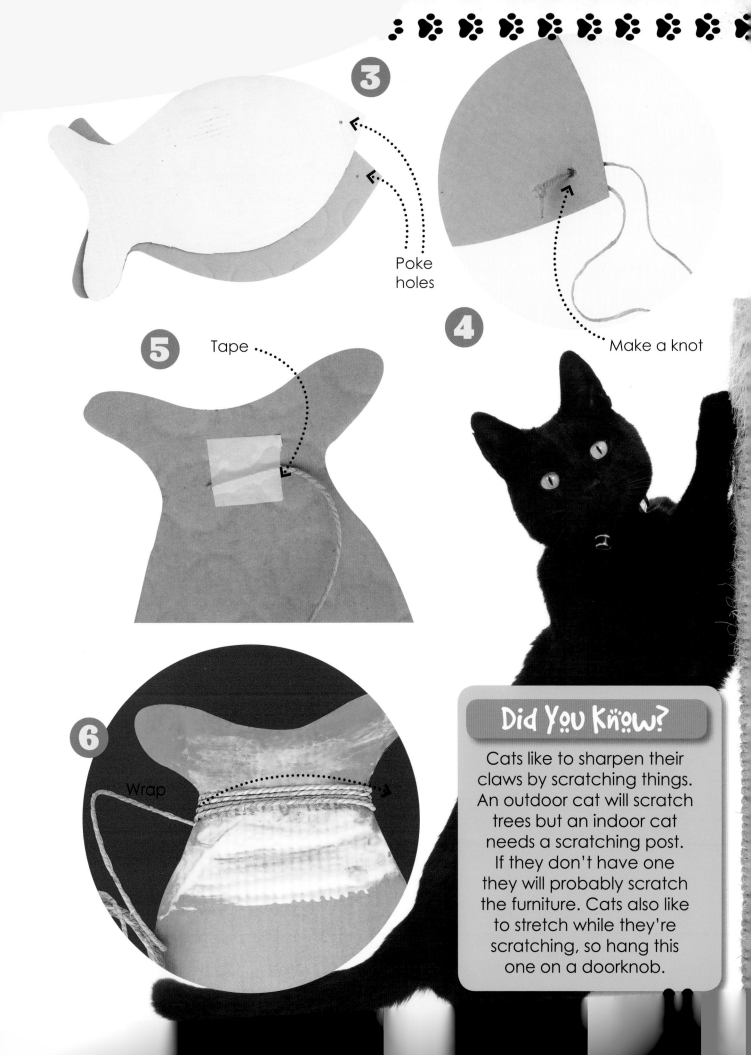

3

Poke holes

4

Make a knot

5

Tape

6

Wrap

Did You Know?

Cats like to sharpen their claws by scratching things. An outdoor cat will scratch trees but an indoor cat needs a scratching post. If they don't have one they will probably scratch the furniture. Cats also like to stretch while they're scratching, so hang this one on a doorknob.

cat frame

Make a special frame for your favorite cat photo by wrapping yarn around a plain frame.

purrfect

meow

Tools & Materials:

- ✔ Plain wood frame
- ✔ White paint and brush (optional)
- ✔ Tape
- ✔ Yarn (**variegated** is shown)

1 Optional: paint your frame white.

2 Tape one end of the ball of yarn to the back of the frame.

3 Start winding the yarn around the frame. Go one way around the frame and then back the other way to make a crisscross pattern. Or just go randomly back and forth.

4 If you run out of yarn or want to change color, tape the end of the yarn to the back of the frame and tape a new piece to the frame.

5 You can leave it sparsely covered or keep winding until the entire frame is covered.

6 Tape a photo to the back. Cut a small piece of yarn and tie each end to the top of the frame to make a loop to hang the frame.

2 Tape

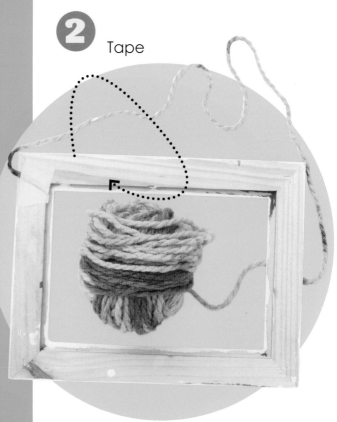

Wind

3

4

Tape

6 Tie

Treat Jar

Make jars to store cat treats in or give as a gift—or even to store your own treats or treasures in!

Tools & Materials:

- ✔ Glue
- ✔ Plastic or paper cup
- ✔ Acrylic paint and brush
- ✔ Cat wrapping paper, fabric, or magazines
- ✔ Paper-mache glue
- ✔ String or ribbon
- ✔ Cardboard
- ✔ Scissors and nail

1. Pour a small amount of glue into a plastic or paper cup. Add some paint. Stir. Add more paint until you are happy with the color. (The glue helps the paint stick to the jar.)

2. Paint the jar and leave to dry.

3. Select your images. Cut up cat wrapping paper, fabric, or magazines. Prepare a small bowl of paper-mache glue. (See page 6.)

4. Apply some glue to the jar. Press an image onto the glue. Smooth out. Repeat with each image you want to put on the jar.

5. Brush paper-mache glue over the entire jar and leave to dry.

6. Cover the top of the lid as you did the jar. Brush glue around the side of the lid. Wrap string or ribbon around the lid.

7. Make a label. Cut out a fish or rectangle shape from cardboard. Glue cut-out words to the cardboard. Punch a hole at the top. Attach to the jar with string.

2

Paint the jar

3

Cut images

4

Glue images

meow

meow

meow

Another IDEA!

Use cat stickers and letter stickers to cover your treat jar. Paint the jar and lid. Leave to dry. Press the stickers to the jar. Cover with a layer of paper-mache glue. Leave to dry. (It works best with thin stickers.)

cat treats

Did You Know?

Don't turn your cat into a fat cat with too many treats! Store them safely in this jar so your cat can't help itself to treats. When it is treat time, shake the jar and give your kitty a few treats.

Treats

6

Glue images

7

meow meow meow

Punch hole

Glue string

fleece Ball

Make cute fleece balls for your cat to play with. Cats love to chase and pounce on balls.

Tools & Materials:

- ✔ Fleece fabric (new or reused from an old blanket or sweater)
- ✔ Scissors and ruler
- ✔ Thick cardboard 3 inches (8 cm) wide by 5 inches (13 cm) long
- ✔ Bell
- ✔ 16-inch (41 cm) piece of string

1 Cut five strips of fleece, 1 inch (3 cm) × 12 inches (30 cm) long.

2 Wrap a strip around the cardboard.

3 Wrap another strip around the first one. Continue wrapping until all five are wrapped around the cardboard.

4 Slip the fleece strips off the cardboard.

5 Thread the string through the bell's opening. Tie it and knot it in the middle of the string.

6 Tie the string around the center of the strips as tightly as you can and knot it. Wrap it around the strips and tie and knot it again.

7 Cut the ends on one end. Cut a couple at a time. It is too thick to cut them all at once. Repeat for the other end.

8 Trim the ends of the strings. Pull the fleece pieces apart and fluff. You can trim the ends of the fleece to make a less floppy ball (like the top ball in the large photo) if you want.

1

Cut 5 strips

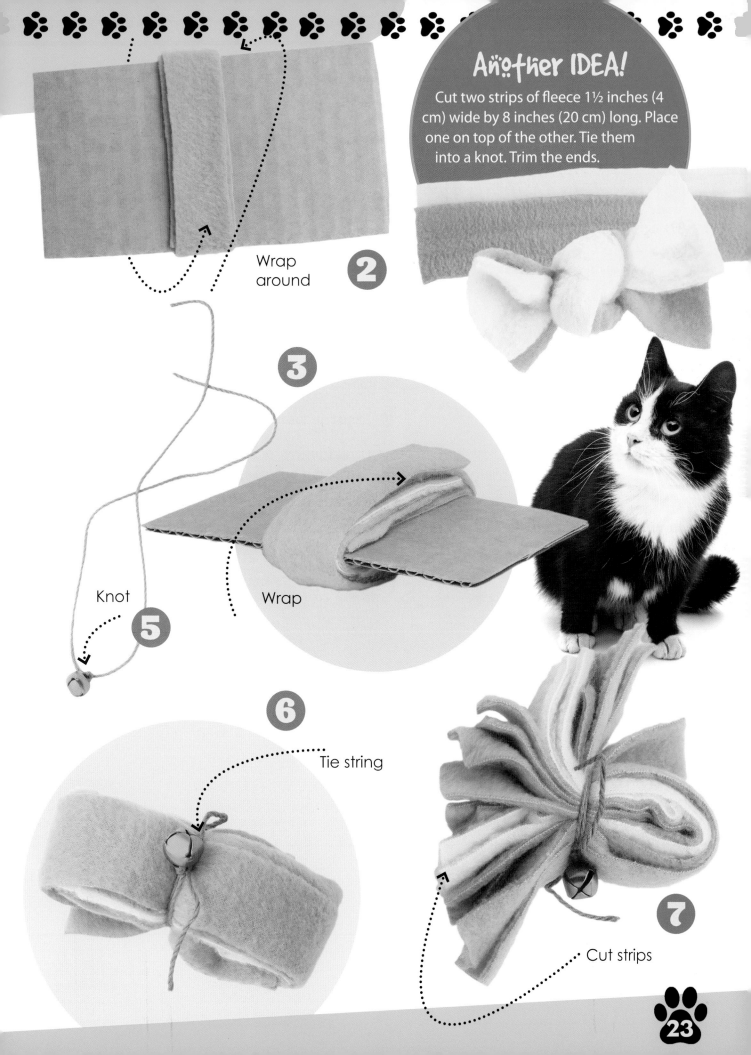

Wrap
around

2

Another IDEA!

Cut two strips of fleece 1½ inches (4 cm) wide by 8 inches (20 cm) long. Place one on top of the other. Tie them into a knot. Trim the ends.

3

Wrap

Knot

5

6

Tie string

Cut strips

7

23

Cat Grass Planter

Cats love to eat grass. Transform a plain pot into a cat head with grass hair for your furry friend.

Tools & Materials:

✔ Paper, pencil, and scissors
✔ Felt (2 colors)
✔ Tape and glue
✔ Yarn or thread and needle
✔ 3 pipe cleaners 8 inches (20 cm) long
✔ 4 ½-inch (11 cm) pot
✔ 2 buttons

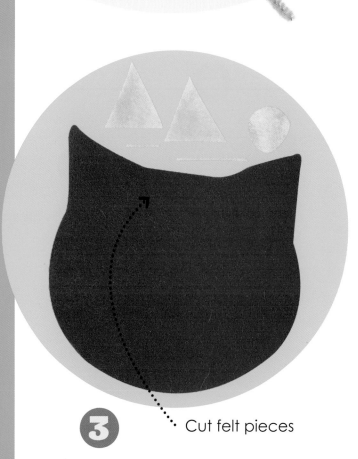

1. Trace the template of head, nose, and ears on page 31 onto a piece of paper. Cut the pieces out.

2. Tape the paper to the felt. The head should be one color and the inner ears and nose a contrasting color.

3. Cut the felt pieces out and remove the pattern. Cut two small narrow pieces of the contrast felt for the mouth.

4. Glue the ears to the head.

5. Sew the buttons to the head for the eyes. Cut two small slits in the felt just below the eyes.

6. Twist the three pipe cleaners together in the center. Pull the pipe cleaners through the slits in the felt. Go under the first slit on the right and then up and through the slit on the left.

7. Glue the nose and mouth to the head. Glue the felt head to the pot.

3

Cut felt pieces

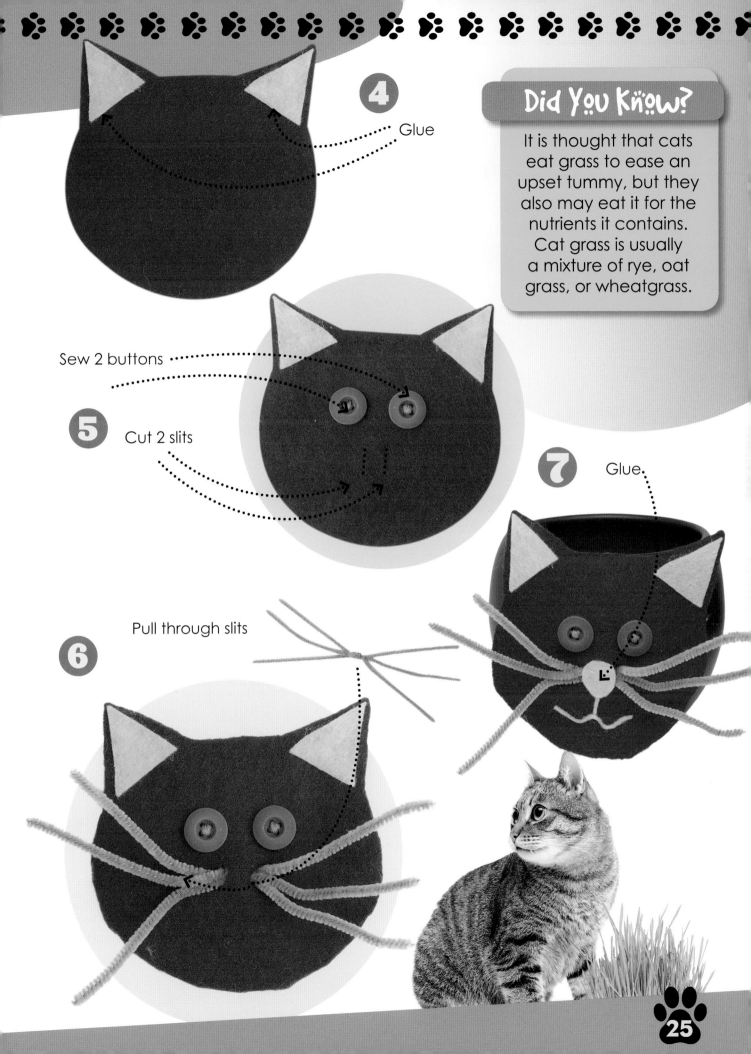

4

Glue

Sew 2 buttons

5 Cut 2 slits

7 Glue

6 Pull through slits

Catnip Pillow

Make a catnip pillow for your cat to sleep on. The catnip will attract the cat to the pillow.

Tools & Materials:

✔ Craft paper or paper bag
✔ Scissors and ruler
✔ Fabric
✔ Sewing needle and thread
✔ Fabric stuffing
✔ Catnip

1. Make a paper pattern by cutting a paper bag or craft paper into a rectangle of 12 inches (30 cm) × 16 inches (41 cm).

2. Cut your fabric to 13 inches (33 cm) × 24 inches (61 cm). There will be an extra ½ inch (1 cm) on either side of the pattern. This is called a **seam allowance**.

3. Fold the fabric over the pattern with the **wrong side** facing out. Fold the two end pieces over. There is extra material so that one end overlaps the other.

4. Slip the pattern out. Sew along one side, ½ inch (1 cm) from the edge. Sew along the other side ½ inch (1 cm) from the edge. Turn the fabric right side out.

5. Fill with stuffing. You want to make a thin pillow shape with it. Sprinkle some catnip on the stuffing.

6. Sew the opening closed using the overcast stitch.

1

2

Cut fabric

3

Turn wrong side out

Another IDEA!

Make a tiny version as a toy. Cut the fabric in a small rectangle or square. Follow steps 4 and 5. Insert stuffing, paper, or crinkling plastic and catnip. Sew shut.

Sew ....

4

Sew ....

Did You Know?

Cats spend their time eating, playing, and sleeping—and they sleep a lot! Cats can sleep up to 20 hours a day. Some are much more active and only sleep for 16 hours.

5 Insert stuffing

6 Sew opening closed

27

Bow Tie

Dress your cat up with a fancy bow tie.

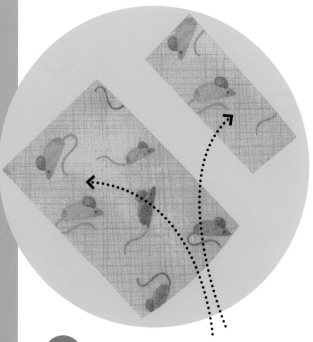

Tools & Materials:

✔ Paper, pencil, and scissors
✔ Fabric
✔ Glue
✔ Paper clip

1 Trace the patterns on page 31 (bow tie A, bow tie B, bow tie C) onto a piece of paper and cut out.

2 Use bow tie A and C patterns to cut two pieces of fabric.

3 Place the large piece of fabric right side down. Lay the bow tie B pattern on top. Spread glue on the paper. Fold the sides of the fabric over the paper. Fold the top of the fabric over. Spread a bit of glue on the folded pieces of fabric. Fold the last piece over. Smooth with your fingers.

4 Pinch the fabric in the middle. Use a paper clip to hold the pinch in place and leave to dry.

5 Remove the paper clip from the large piece of fabric. Wrap the small strip of fabric around it. Apply some glue to the small strip where it overlaps. Use the paper clip to hold it in place until dry.

6 Slip a cat collar through the fabric ring.

2 Cut fabric rectangles

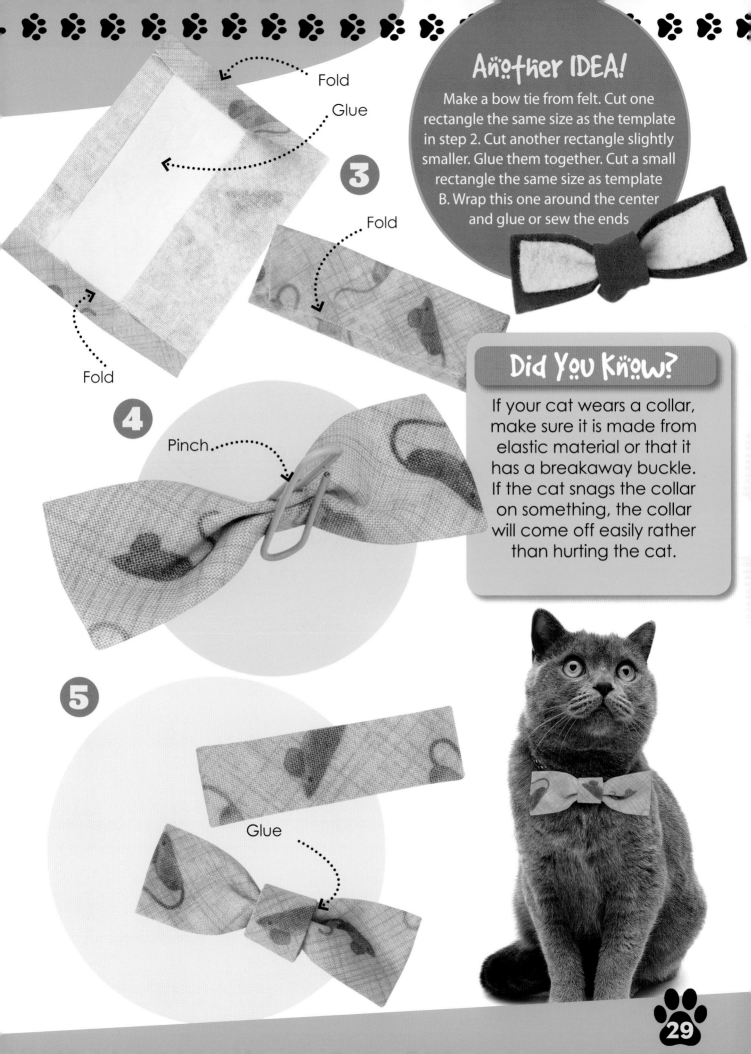

Fold

Glue

Fold

Fold

3

Fold

4

Pinch

5

Glue

Glue

Did You Know?

If your cat wears a collar, make sure it is made from elastic material or that it has a breakaway buckle. If the cat snags the collar on something, the collar will come off easily rather than hurting the cat.

Patterns

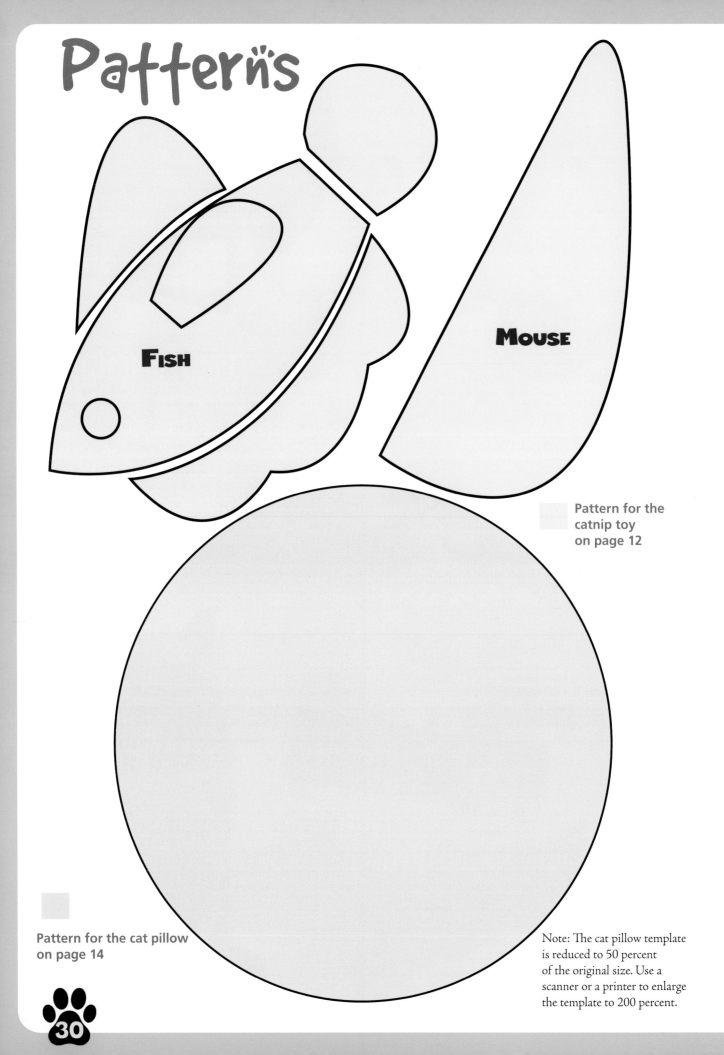

FISH

MOUSE

Pattern for the
catnip toy
on page 12

Pattern for the cat pillow
on page 14

Note: The cat pillow template
is reduced to 50 percent
of the original size. Use a
scanner or a printer to enlarge
the template to 200 percent.

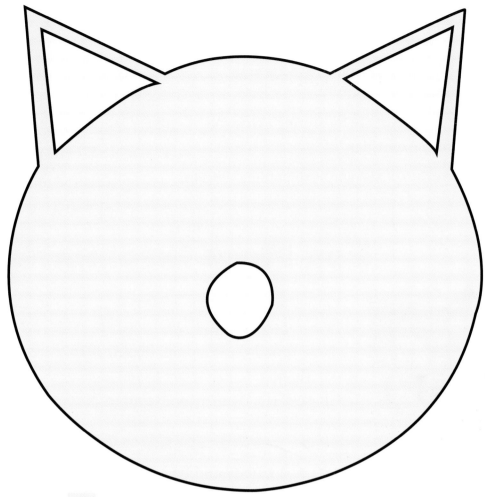

Pattern for the cat grass planter on page 24

A

B

C

Pattern for the bow tie on page 28

31

GLOSSARY

domesticated Adapted to living with humans.

hope chest A space for storing items you hope to use someday.

perseverance Keeping at something despite difficulties.

right side The printed or top side of fabric.

seam allowance The area between the edge of the fabric and the stitching.

variegated Having a variety of colors.

wrong side The underside or nonprinted side of fabric.

FOR MORE INFORMATION

FURTHER READING

Lim, Annalees. *Pet Crafts.* New York, NY: Windmill Books, 2016.

Thomas, Isabel. *Cool Cat Projects.* Chicago, IL: Heinemann Raintree, 2016.

WEBSITES

Cat Family and Its Members
easyscienceforkids.com/all-about-the-cat-family
Learn more about cats here!

Cats
www.ducksters.com/animals/cats.php
Check out this link to find out more about these great pets.

INDEX